CEREAL
CITY GUIDE
LOS ANGELES

ABRAMS IMAGE,
NEW YORK

A City Guide by CEREAL

Rosa Park, Editor in Chief
Rich Stapleton, Creative Director
Ruth Ainsworth, Sub Editor
Ollie Horne, Assistant Editor
Charlie Cook, Editorial Intern
Lily Dalzell & Molly Cropper,
Producers

Book design by
Studio Faculty

Photography by
Carmen Chan, Justin Chung,
Marissa Marino, Rich Stapleton,
Rick Poon

Words by
Jared Frank, Jenny Bahn,
Libby Borton, Lucy Brook,
Matilda Bathurst, Ollie Horne,
Aslan, Sean Hotchkiss

Illustrations by
Jessica Ng

Editor: Laura Dozier
Managing Editor: Glenn Ramirez
Design Manager: Danny Maloney
Production Manager: Katie Gaffney

Library of Congress Control Number:
2020931087

ISBN: 978-1-4197-4715-1
eISBN: 978-1-68335-998-2

Printed and bound in China
10 9 8 7 6 5 4 3 2 1

Abrams books are available at special discounts when
purchased in quantity for premiums and promotions as well
as fundraising or educational use. Special editions can also
be created to specification. For details, contact
specialsales@abramsbooks.com or the address below.

ABRAMS The Art of Books
195 Broadway, New York, NY 10007
abramsbooks.com

We, at Cereal, have traveled to cities around the world and sought out places we believe to be unique, interesting, and enjoyable. Our aim is to produce guides that would befit Cereal readers and modern travelers alike, recommending a tightly edited selection of experiences that combine quality with meticulous design. If the food is top-notch, so too is the space that accompanies it. You'll soon notice that our version of the perfect trip is woven in with an understated flair and a penchant for grand landscapes, both natural and constructed. Within these pages, you will find the practical advice you need on where to stay, where to eat, what to see, and where to shop.

This guide to Los Angeles features a considered selection of shops, hotels, restaurants, cafés, and points of interest. Not intending to be comprehensive, we present a discerning edit of our favorite places to visit in the city.

All photographs, copy, and illustrations are original and exclusive to Cereal.

While all information in this book was accurate at the time of printing, please call venues before visiting to confirm that nothing has changed.

CONTENTS

A City Guide by CEREAL

INTERVIEWS

ESSAYS

ADDITIONAL INFORMATION

LOS ANGELES

Watch something on screen, be it at the movies, on TV or even on your smartphone, and the chances are that the content was made in Los Angeles. Show business is big business; the city turns over more than 800 billion US dollars a year, dwarfing the output of many nation states. Out on the palm-fringed western edge of the American dream, the City of Angels is everything you imagine it to be; glamorous, glitzy, and hungry for fame. It might be expressways, beaches, and beautiful people you notice first, but it's the city's energy you'll remember.

COUNTRY	USA
AIRPORT	LAX
LANGUAGE	ENGLISH
CURRENCY	USD
DIALING CODE	+1

A PHOTO ESSAY

photos by RICH STAPLETON

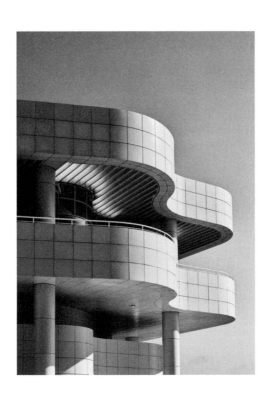

NEIGHBORHOODS

MAP
of LOS ANGELES

<table>
<tr><td>1</td><td>Pacific Palisades</td><td>19</td><td>Cheviot Hills</td><td>37</td><td>Mid-City</td></tr>
<tr><td>2</td><td>Santa Monica</td><td>20</td><td>Beverlywood</td><td>38</td><td>Arlington Heights</td></tr>
<tr><td>3</td><td>Venice</td><td>21</td><td>Palms</td><td>39</td><td>Harvard Heights</td></tr>
<tr><td>4</td><td>Marina del Rey</td><td>22</td><td>Culver City</td><td>40</td><td>Pico-Union</td></tr>
<tr><td>5</td><td>Playa Vista</td><td>23</td><td>Ladera Heights</td><td>41</td><td>Westlake</td></tr>
<tr><td>6</td><td>Del Rey</td><td>24</td><td>Carthay</td><td>42</td><td>Rampart Village</td></tr>
<tr><td>7</td><td>Mar Vista</td><td>25</td><td>Beverly Grove</td><td>43</td><td>Silver Lake</td></tr>
<tr><td>8</td><td>Sawtelle</td><td>26</td><td>West Hollywood</td><td>44</td><td>Los Feliz</td></tr>
<tr><td>9</td><td>Veterans Administration</td><td>27</td><td>Hollywood Hills West</td><td>45</td><td>Griffith Park</td></tr>
<tr><td>10</td><td>Brentwood</td><td>28</td><td>Hollywood Hills</td><td>46</td><td>Glassell Park</td></tr>
<tr><td>11</td><td>Bel Air</td><td>29</td><td>Hollywood</td><td>47</td><td>Elysian Valley</td></tr>
<tr><td>12</td><td>Beverly Crest</td><td>30</td><td>East Hollywood</td><td>48</td><td>Elysian Park</td></tr>
<tr><td>13</td><td>Westwood</td><td>31</td><td>Fairfax</td><td>49</td><td>Echo Park</td></tr>
<tr><td>14</td><td>Beverly Hills</td><td>32</td><td>Hancock Park</td><td>50</td><td>Chinatown</td></tr>
<tr><td>15</td><td>West Los Angeles</td><td>33</td><td>Larchmont</td><td>51</td><td>Downtown</td></tr>
<tr><td>16</td><td>Century City</td><td>34</td><td>Windsor Square</td><td>52</td><td>Malibu</td></tr>
<tr><td>17</td><td>South Robertson</td><td>35</td><td>Koreatown</td><td>53</td><td>Highland Park</td></tr>
<tr><td>18</td><td>Rancho Park</td><td>36</td><td>Mid-Wilshire</td><td>54</td><td>San Marino</td></tr>
</table>

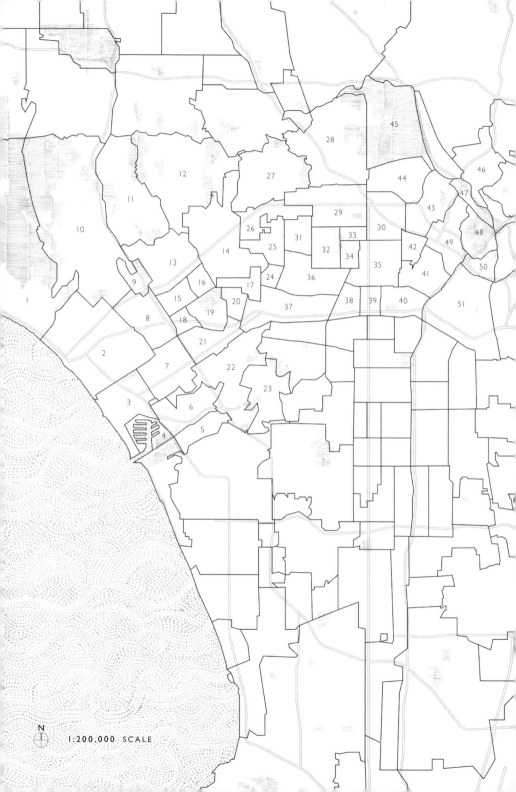

N
1:200,000 SCALE

SANTA MONICA PROPER HOTEL

HOTEL
in SANTA MONICA

In a Spanish Colonial Revival building on Wilshire Boulevard, Kelly Wearstler's design for Santa Monica Proper Hotel recalls the golden tones and textures of the California coast, from sand-engrained paintings to sun-shaped headboards. The hotel stands out for its generously proportioned rooms, Ayurvedic Surya spa, and complimentary yoga classes for guests.

+1 310-620-9990
properhotel.com/hotels/santa-monica

700 Wilshire Blvd
Santa Monica, CA 90401

VILLA CARLOTTA

It's easy to feel at home in one of Villa Carlotta's self-catered apartments. Available for stays of thirty days or longer, the studios, one-bed and two-bed suites often attract a clientele of actors and musicians. Each of the residences in this restored historic monument combines Parisian style and Old Hollywood glamour, with pink and teal sofas, ornate balustrades and archways, and hand-stenciled coffered ceilings. While Franklin Village bustles outside, the villa's palm garden and heated saltwater pool provide a restful haven. As the sun sets, head to the rooftop to enjoy a movie, or to take in the view of the Hollywood sign as it lights up the hillside.

+1 323-628-6628
villacarlottala.com

5959 Franklin Ave
Los Angeles, CA 90028

VILLA CARLOTTA HOTEL

THE SURFRIDER

HOTEL
in MALIBU

On the famed Pacific Coast Highway, overlooking its namesake beach, the Surfrider possesses all the ease of a modern Californian beach house. Occupying a classic 1950s former motel, its twenty intimate rooms open onto balconies hung with hammocks; palms and olives dot the interiors, and an outdoor terrace overlooks the Pacific coast and Malibu Pier. Flanked by the Santa Monica Mountains to the rear, The Surfrider is perfectly placed to enjoy hiking trails, waves, and the pristine Californian light.

+1 310-526-6158
thesurfridermalibu.com

23033 Pacific Coast Hwy
Malibu, CA 90265

SILVER LAKE
POOL & INN

HOTEL
in SILVER LAKE

Striped umbrellas and poolside cocktails encapsulate the experience at Silver Lake Pool & Inn, a revitalized former motel with a playful, nostalgic atmosphere. While the rooms are impeccably designed, furnished with low leather armchairs and terrazzo side tables, and stocked with local mezcal, the pool is the main event— even the name of the on-site Italian restaurant, Marco Polo, is reminiscent of the classic childhood pool game. Positioned just south of Sunset Junction, the hotel brings the laid-back calm of the coast to East LA.

+1 323-486-7225

palisociety.com/hotels/silverlake

4141 Santa Monica Boulevard
Los Angeles, CA 90026

CHATEAU MARMONT

Mythos emanates from the halls of Chateau Marmont. Things are always happening within the walls of this seven-story castle on a hill, designed after the Château d'Amboise in the Loire Valley: raucous parties by the pool; celebrity sightings at Bar Marmont; late-night trysts in Bungalow 3. A haven for the city's creatively inclined, this West Hollywood landmark has become synonymous with indulgence, debauchery, and anonymity. Life at the Chateau is predictable, but never boring.

+1 323-656-1010
chateaumarmont.com

8221 Sunset Blvd
Los Angeles, CA 90046

FELIX TRATTORIA

RESTAURANT
in VENICE

Traditional Italian cooking finds a Californian home in Felix Trattoria. With twenty years of expertise behind him, Evan Funke transforms local Californian ingredients into irresistible Italian fare, crafting fleets of delicate handmade pasta in a temperature-controlled, glass-paned kitchen. The ever-changing pasta menu, organized by region of origin, may include pappardelle, *foglie d'ulivo*, or orecchiette, and is accompanied by classic antipasti and pizzas. A highlight is the salty *focaccia siciliana*, flecked with rosemary sprigs and drizzled in olive oil.

+1 424-387-8622
felixla.com

1023 Abbot Kinney Blvd
Los Angeles, CA 90291

KISMET

Co-chefs Sara Kramer and Sarah Hymanson blend Middle Eastern and Californian flavors from breakfast to dinner at Kismet. Located on the edge of Los Feliz with its attractive pink neon sign, the restaurant is long and narrow, clad and furnished in soft-toned wood. The vegetable-focused menu is meant to be enjoyed family-style, so come prepared to share jeweled crispy rice with plates of spiced carrots and chickpeas, green and yellow beans in sunflower-seed tahini, and buttery Tokyo turnips.

+1 323-409-0404
kismetlosangeles.com

4648 Hollywood Blvd
Los Angeles, CA 90027

MAJORDŌMO

Majordōmo is the first restaurant in LA from the founder of Momofuku, David Chang, and serves Californian cuisine, informed by the diverse culinary culture of the city. Soft, chewy *bing* flatbreads come with spicy lamb or eggs and smoked roe, and tempura-style fried peppers are stuffed with sausage. Unusual twists appear, too, such as short ribs braised with Asian pear and daikon and topped with melted raclette cheese. If you are in a group, preorder the smoked pork shoulder ahead of your arrival to enjoy across the table with kimchi fried rice and *banchan*.

+1 323-545-4880
majordomo.la

1725 Naud St
Los Angeles, CA, 90012

WOON

Keegan Fong had a dream of setting up a restaurant to share the recipes his mother, Julie (also fondly known as Mama Fong), cooked throughout his childhood. From its beginnings as a noodle cart and pop-up operation, family-run Woon has grown into a fully fledged restaurant near Historic Filipinotown, and still serves the same great home-style Chinese cooking. Share *bao*, noodles, fried rice with sweet Chinese sausage, and wok-tossed spicy potato chips in this casual setting.

+1 213-674-7434
woonkitchen.com

2920 W Temple St
Los Angeles, CA 90026

PINE & CRANE

RESTAURANT
in SILVER LAKE

Chef and owner Vivian Ku wanted a place to serve the food she grew up with. Enter Pine & Crane—the fast, casual Taiwanese-Chinese restaurant in Silver Lake that serves up hot bowls of *zha jiang* noodles, mapo tofu, and three-cup Jidori chicken every day of the week except Tuesdays. You don't have to fly across the Pacific for authentic Taiwanese-Chinese cuisine at affordable prices: pull up to Griffith Park Boulevard, wait in line, and grab a seat at Pine & Crane.

+1 323-668-1128
pineandcrane.com

1521 Griffith Park Blvd
Los Angeles, CA 90026

JON & VINNY'S

RESTAURANT
in FAIRFAX

Jon & Vinny's, situated in the Fairfax District, opens at 8 a.m., serving pitch-perfect pizzas, pastas, and salads until 10 p.m., seven days a week. Cloaked in white American oak, the cozy interior features raw porcelain sconces from ceramist Shio Kusaka, and the restaurant is filled with a warm and friendly vibe. Jon Shook and Vinny Dotolo, the duo that brought Los Angeles Animal, Son of a Gun, and Trois Mec, strike gold again with their unique take on classic Italian dishes. There are only forty-five seats inside, so make sure to get a reservation. And if you find yourself further west, check out their second spot on San Vicente Boulevard in Brentwood, which opened in 2019.

+1 323-334-3369
jonandvinnys.com

412 N Fairfax Ave
Los Angeles, CA 90036

KONBI

RESTAURANT
in ECHO PARK

If you stroll down Sunset Boulevard you may happen upon Konbi, a narrow, daytime restaurant in Echo Park. Grab a seat at the ten-stool bar for a specialty Hojicha latte and a croissant, or try one of their celebrated sandwiches, served between soft Japanese milk bread. The crunchy pork katsu sandwich is a particular favorite, as is the egg salad, mixed with a hint of Dijon. But if sandwiches aren't your thing, Konbi offers an excellent selection of vegetable-based small plates, such as locally made Meiji tofu, served with dashi, ginger, and buckwheat.

+1 213-278-0007
konbila.com

1463 Sunset Blvd
Los Angeles, CA 90026

MARU COFFEE

The quiet, contemplative space of Maru is ideal for sipping your morning coffee. Jacob Park and Joonmo Kim opened their first shop in Los Feliz, followed by this larger location in Arts District. The name "Maru" is derived from an old Korean word, *san ma ru*, meaning "mountaintop," in reference to the higher altitudes that often yield the best coffee. Maru offers an extensive range of roasts, and serves pour overs, espressos, and lattes in cups made by Notary Ceramics.

+1 213-372-5755
marucoffee.com

1019 S Santa Fe Ave
Los Angeles, CA 90021

GALERIE HALF

Art books are stacked atop a nightstand; a pewter teapot sits on a dining table; a gold-framed mirror hangs on the wall. Galerie Half, the modern retail concept from Cameron Smith and Cliff Fong, feels more akin to a home than a place to buy twentieth-century antiques, furniture, and artwork. Situated on Melrose Avenue in Hollywood, the gallery and showroom features a judicious selection of works from the likes of Børge Mogensen, Poul Henningsen, and Jean Royère. As the afternoon light spills in, and the captivating fragrance of a Perfumer H candle fills the air, you may find yourself sitting on the Boesen armchair much longer than you expected.

+1 323-424-3866
galeriehalf.com

6911 Melrose Ave
Los Angeles, CA 90038

SUMNER

Sumner is an approachable space and a pleasure to browse. The proprietor, Jessica Garber, has assembled a collection of humane Scandinavian and French furniture, curvaceous sculptural forms, and the occasional nineteenth-century antique. The cohesive, organic palette of weathered wood, tan leather, and soft whites is persuasive: If you could, you'd simply buy everything and never have to shop again.

+1 818-606-4312
sumnershop.com

6915 Melrose Ave
Los Angeles, CA 90038

COUNTER-SPACE

Fondly subtitled "T-shirts & Chairs," Counter-Space is never constrained by one genre or style. Menswear by in-house brand Lady White Co. creates banners of white and beige beside shelves of incense and fragrance, while mid-century and vintage furnishings are paired with sculptures and pottery in burnished tones.

+1 323-741-8337
counter-space.com

1837 Hyperion Ave
Los Angeles, CA 90027

THE ELDER STATESMAN

APPAREL & ACCESSORIES SHOP
in WEST HOLLYWOOD

The Elder Stateman's West Hollywood store is strewn with exquisite, limited-run cashmere in a cacophony of colors and patterns. With over a decade of experience, founder Greg Chait's brand is renowned for the unrivaled comfort and quality of its sweaters and blankets, which draw artistic collaborators and devoted customers. Think palm tree motifs and hand-dyed fabrics in sunset hues.

Read Greg Chait's essay about LA (see page 168)

+1 424-288-4221
elder-statesman.com

607 Huntley Dr
Los Angeles, CA 90069

THE ROW

APPAREL SHOP
in WEST HOLLYWOOD

There's an unmistakable sense of refinement and acute restraint at The Row. The sparse, 3,770 square-foot space is laden with California sunlight, and features European furniture, vintage jewelry, and garments from the brand's lines of womenswear, menswear, and accessories. Paintings, sculptures, and prints from the Olsens' personal collection are on display, while floor-to-ceiling glass partitions retract for access to a recessed pool in the courtyard. The boutique and its beautiful wares leave patrons longing for the Olsens' way of life.

Cereal talks to Mary-Kate and Ashley Olsen (see page 159)

+1 310-853-1900
therow.com

8440 Melrose Pl
Los Angeles, CA 90069

ARCH THE

A meditative calm characterizes Arch The. Founder and designer Joo Eunsil has created a gallery-like space that unifies the simplicity of Korean aesthetics with Californian lightness and delicacy. The store's most notable quality is tactility, from the soft cottons and cashmeres of sweaters and dresses to rough clay bowls and handwoven baskets.

+1 213-500-8807
archthe.com

711 Mateo St
Los Angeles, CA 90021

LCD

Founded in 2012 by Geraldine Chung, LCD, abbreviated from Lust Covet Desire, is on a mission to uncover and support independent designers worldwide. The keenly researched range of womenswear, beauty, and homewares is influenced by contemporary art and street culture, with each item upholding Chung's uncompromising stance on quality and craftsmanship.

+1 424-280-4132
shoplcd.co

1121 Abbot Kinney Blvd, Suite 2
Los Angeles, CA 90291

SANSO

Sanso is a plant design company that pairs rare flora with handmade stoneware vessels and planters. Taking its name from the Korean word for "oxygen," Sanso sources unusual plants from private collectors, who grow their specimens from seed or cuttings in specialist greenhouses. The team at Sanso craft their own stoneware in their LA studio, which they feature alongside unique pieces by fellow Angelino and ceramic artist Nancy Kwon. If your home requires a breath of fresh air, Sanso has got you covered.

sanso.la

618 Moulton Ave, Suite E
Los Angeles, CA 90031

GENERAL STORE

Follow a brushed concrete floor under a sweeping white archway as you meander through General Store. Shelves and tables are festooned with locally made crafts, found objects and womenswear. The featured independent clothing lines share values such as small-batch production and sustainability, organic materials, and a frank and practical sense of femininity, with many garments produced in California. The range of homewares is similarly well-chosen, delighting in beauty and functionality, and including stoneware vases, hand-carved utensils, and fair trade textiles.

+1 310-751-6393
shop-generalstore.com

1801 Lincoln Blvd
Los Angeles, CA 90291

TORTOISE GENERAL STORE

HOMEWARES SHOP
in MAR VISTA

Under rusted tin awnings, Tortoise General Store is a utilitarian space, stocked floor to ceiling with thoughtful Japanese homewares designed to improve your every day, from clocks to shoes, bowls to jewelry, and clothes to small wooden figurines. After a visit to Hawaii, owners Keiko and Taku Shinomoto were inspired to bring the spirit of a traditional general store to LA, opening on Abbot Kinney before relocating to Mar Vista in 2018. Now expanded into the adjacent two units, the Tortoise gallery stocks furniture, art, and vintage pieces, and Tortoise Hasami Porcelain Store features Taku Shinomoto's original designs, made in Hasami, Japan.

+1 310-396-7335
tortoiselife.com

12701 Venice Blvd
Los Angeles, CA 90066

ARCANA: BOOKS ON THE ARTS

BOOK SHOP
in CULVER CITY

Located in the historic Helms Bakery building, Arcana: Books on the Arts continues to serve the Los Angeles community as it has since 1984. Its collection includes over one hundred thousand rare and out-of-print books on twentieth- and twenty-first-century art, architecture, design, and photography.

+1 310-458-1499
arcanabooks.com

8675 Washington Blvd
Culver City, CA 90232

OWL BUREAU

Owl Bureau is the brainchild of Richard Christiansen, whose agency, Chandelier Creative, lives behind this highly curated bookstore. Perforated plywood shelves support rows of rare books that shed a light on Christiansen's inspirations and obsessions. While some longtime residents of gentrifying Highland Park might prefer an affordable bookstore, Owl makes the case that in the Amazon era, a creative community centered around books you would never find online is more valuable than another mass-market paperback.

+1 424-285-5517
chandeliercreative.com

5634 N Figueroa St
Los Angeles, CA 90042

HOLLYHOCK HOUSE

POINT OF INTEREST
in EAST HOLLYWOOD

Cresting Olive Hill in Barnsdall Art Park like a crown, Frank Lloyd Wright's Hollyhock House glows in honey-colored stone. Built between 1919 and 1921 for Aline Barnsdall, the building was awarded UNESCO World Heritage status in 2019. It features many of Lloyd Wright's classic architectural signatures, such as vast windows, an open-plan living space, bold lines, and geometric accents. Mayan architectural shapes embellish the walls, from the numerous roof terraces down to the patio.

+1 323-988-0516
barnsdall.org/hollyhock-house

4800 Hollywood Blvd
Los Angeles, CA 90027

THE GETTY

MUSEUM
in BRENTWOOD

+1 310-440-7300
getty.edu

1200 Getty Center Dr
Los Angeles, CA 90049

Take the three-car tram up the long incline of Los Angeles's Brentwood neighborhood, and arrive on top of the Getty Center. Celebrated for its geometric architecture, gardens, and expansive vistas overlooking the city, the museum is one of LA's most recognized cultural institutions. Designed by Pritzker Prize–winning architect Richard Meier, it houses a collection of artworks from the J. Paul Getty Trust.

GRIFFITH OBSERVATORY

The Griffith Observatory is one of the most visited tourist attractions in town—and it earns that distinction with good reason. This grand Art Deco icon perched on the slopes of Mount Hollywood offers stunning views over the city to the south and the Hollywood sign to the west. Alternatively, turn your gaze to the stars with one of the planetarium's shows, or via the observatory's telescopes.

+1 213-473-0800
griffithobservatory.org

2800 E Observatory Rd
Los Angeles, CA 90027

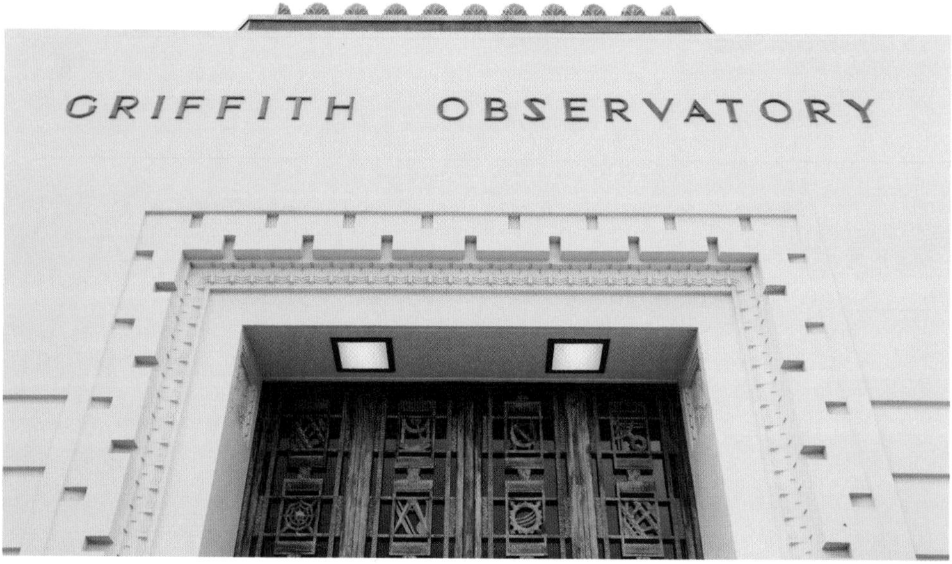
GRIFFITH OBSERVATORY

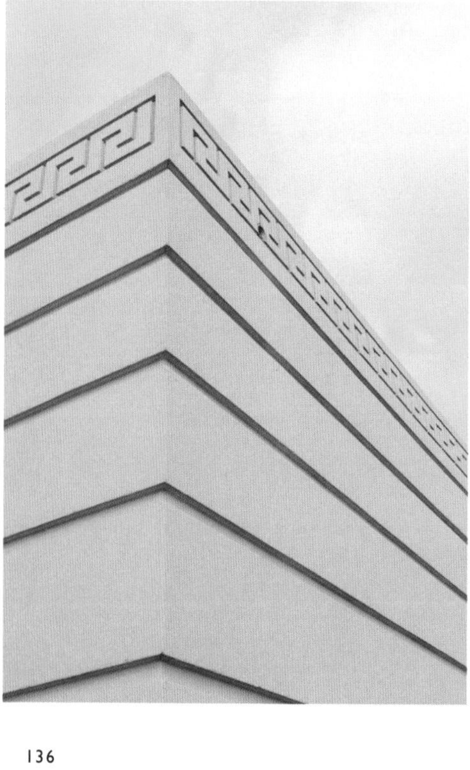

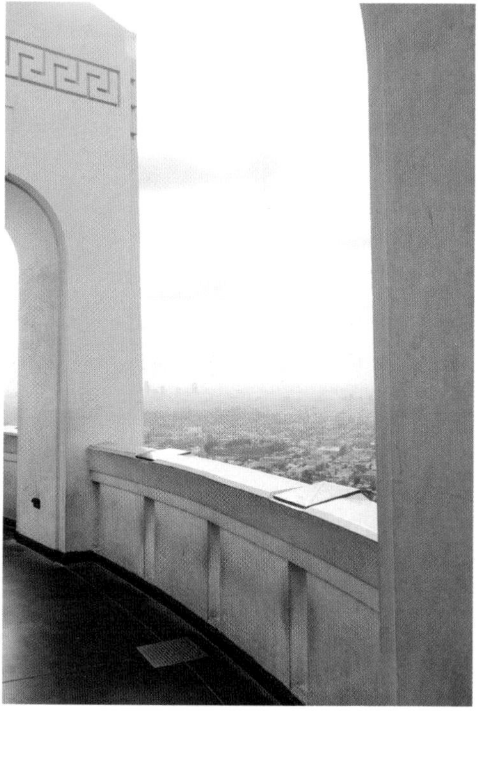

HUNTINGTON BOTANICAL GARDENS

GARDEN & MUSEUM
in SAN MARINO

.

Huntington Botanical Gardens sprawl over 120 acres populated with thousands of plant varieties. Each of the sixteen gardens has its own ecosystem, from that of desert succulents and cacti to fragrant roses and maples. The Californian, Japanese, and Chinese gardens each encapsulate elements of their respective cultures, with water features, moon bridges, and pavilions. Wander leisurely, and lose yourself among the borders.

+1 626-405-2100
huntington.org

1151 Oxford Rd
San Marino, CA 91108

STAHL HOUSE

For design enthusiasts everywhere, the Stahl House (completed in 1960) is, without a doubt, one of the most iconic symbols of mid-century modern architecture in Los Angeles. Nestled in the Hollywood Hills with panoramic views, Pierre Koenig's Case Study House #22 is dramatic yet understated, much like the city it looks out over. The house is only open by reservation; book onto one of the three tours, held between midday and sunset.

+1 208-429-1058
stahlhouse.com

1635 Woods Dr
Los Angeles, CA 90069

THE BROAD

ADDITIONAL RECOMMENDATIONS

PALIHOUSE SANTA MONICA *Hotel | palisociety.com*

HOTEL 850 SVB *Hotel | hotel850svb.com*

CARA HOTEL *Hotel | carahotel.com*

BREADBLOK *Bakery | breadblok.com*

ALL TIME *Restaurant | alltimelosangeles.com*

JOY *Restaurant | joyonyork.com*

HIPPO *Restaurant | hipporestaurant.com*

NEEDLE *Restaurant | needlela.com*

THE GOOD LIVER *Homewares Shop | good-liver.com*

MIXED BUSINESS *Womenswear Shop | mixedbusinessla.com*

NEW HIGH MART *Homewares Shop | newhighmart.com*

OLDERBROTHER *Apparel Shop | olderbrother.us*

SHAINA MOTE *Apparel Shop | shainamote.com*

MOHAWK GENERAL STORE *Apparel & Accessories Shop | mohawkgeneralstore.com*

LACMA *Art Museum | lacma.org*

THE BROAD *Art Museum | thebroad.org*

CASA PERFECT *Gallery | thefutureperfect.com*

OLDERBROTHER   PALIHOUSE SANTA MONICA

LACMA

INTERVIEWS

For Amanda Chantal Bacon, the founder and owner of Moon Juice, LA was meant to be a stopover, a place to hone her culinary skills before embarking on further travels; instead, she has found a home here. Her stores are cult destinations for a spectrum of plant- and mushroom-sourced supplements, tonics, and snacks, and her signature well-being and beauty-enhancing dusts.

CEREAL: How did you come to call Los Angeles home?

AMANDA CHANTAL BACON: It was the fruits and vegetables that brought me to LA. I moved here via South America and Vermont, where I'd been at culinary school, to work for one of my mentors, chef and restaurateur Suzanne Goin. I never intended to stay. I've lived here since 2004, and I'm just starting to hit what feels like a sustainable groove in this city.

I was born and raised in Manhattan, so Los Angeles feels more like a bunch of smaller towns, strung together by highways and sprawl. Trying to approach it as a traditional city kept me in years of frustration. You can't walk anywhere, and the traffic is tremendous. What makes LA work for me is nature. I have one day a week where I can slow down and get into real time. I put the phone off, I don't get in the car, I use my two feet, and I look around. Using the nature around us has made such a big difference, and made this a place I could really begin to call home.

CEREAL: Which natural areas in particular do you find solace in?

ACB: I live in Rustic Canyon. My wish was to move somewhere I could walk out the door and into the trees. Around my house, there

AMANDA CHANTAL BACON INTERVIEW

are trails that wind through the landscape. My husband surfs—surf beaches aren't always the most beautiful, but I love Heaven's Beach, where you can take stairs down a cliff to the sand, and Third Point, where there's a little boardwalk you can access through protected marshlands. When the tide is out, I can walk for miles.

CEREAL: What about LA inspires you, and how does that feed into your creativity?

ACB: When I used to visit LA, the mistake I always made was to show up with a car and hit the streets, whereas the true beauty of LA is the interior. It's all the things you can't see from the street, and you can't necessarily access from a car, whether that's nature—going on a hike, spending time at the beach—or going to a friend's place and seeing the wonderful things they have done with their home and garden. A lot of my inspiration comes from the grounding and the silence I can find here, and the mind-bending natural places within a short drive of the city. I always encourage people to get out when they visit, to hire a camper van and go to Joshua Tree or Big Sur, or just take a couple of days, go up to the coast and camp.

CEREAL: What about some of your favorite places to spend time in the city?

ACB: There's a lot to love in the city. The original Jon & Vinny's is in Fairfax, but I go to the one in Brentwood. It's incredible for breakfast, lunch, and dinner. Farmshop has produce from some of the best farmers in California; there's a great coffee bar, and the restaurant does amazing food. On the East Side, there's a market I love called Cookbook—it's a snug little grocery brimming with locally grown produce—and Solar Return, a bakery that makes rainbow vegan cheesecakes. Each cake is a piece of art.

For shopping, I love Tortoise General Store, a Japanese shop on the West Side, as well as General Store in Venice, and Midland in Culver City, which sell beautiful, organic, handmade Californian crafts. And I adore Dôen. The store is in the same location as Farmshop, so for an ultimate moment, you could have breakfast or brunch at

Farmshop then go to Dôen and try on dresses. For health and beauty, my favorite places are Ricari Studios for lymphatic drainage massage, and I love going to Striiike, where my friend Kristie Streicher is the brow guru of LA.

CEREAL: How would you describe Los Angeles to someone who has never visited?

ACB: I think in the last few years there's been a real opening in LA. It's more wellness oriented now, and people come here to be happy and take care of themselves. A lot of people move here from New York or other big metropolises to have a different life story. It's a place for nature, health, and happiness.

———

MOONJUICE.COM

THE ROW: AN INTERVIEW WITH MARY-KATE & ASHLEY OLSEN

words by MATILDA BATHURST
photos by RICH STAPLETON

There is something very intentional about entering The Row. Set back from the street, the store is accessed via a stone atrium, which leads towards a tall glass door. This is not a place that is discovered by chance; only a certain few will recognize the letters etched into the bronze handle, and think to push the door and enter.

Before catching sight of the garments displayed on either side of the store, you see the raised pool in the central courtyard—loungers and towels are arranged for invisible swimmers, and there is a sense of having entered a private home. Either that, or you have trespassed into another world entirely—a dream walk-in-wardrobe, extending across a continuum from loungewear to eveningwear.

This atmosphere of privacy and good taste, of exuberance and reticence, reflects the ethos of The Row's founders, Mary-Kate and Ashley Olsen. When they established the brand in 2006, the two women made the conscious decision to maintain a low profile: It was important that the clothes should speak for themselves—a language of draped silhouettes and sculpted lines, rigorous tailoring and graceful ease.

When they opened their Los Angeles store in 2014, it was a homecoming of sorts. "We were born and raised in Los Angeles, and we used to spend a lot of time on Melrose Place," explains Mary-Kate. "We've seen the city grow and evolve," says Ashley. "It's becoming much more international, and more attention is being paid to architecture and culture. The store was formerly a Sally Hershberger salon, and we would come here when we were children. There is a sense of personal history for us here."

See page 98 for information on The Row

In collaboration with the LA-based architect David Montalba and the interior designer Courtney Applebaum, they sought to capture the essence of California Modernism—an interweaving of inside and out, where uncluttered interior spaces open onto intimate courtyards of native trees and desert plants. As such, the store forms part of the larger narrative of the West Hollywood neighborhood, a testing ground for Modernist architects like Rudolph Schindler and Richard Neutra. "The flow of the space was very important, so our first decision was to incorporate the glass walls," says Ashley. "We wanted the store to feel as open and visible as possible, and to reflect aspects of LA, not just within the architecture, but also within the curation and offering." "When we opened the Los Angeles store, everything was sourced locally," adds Mary-Kate. "Los Angeles has so many wonderful galleries, and there are more than ever before. The gallery Kayne Griffin Corcoran helped us to design the space, and we were advised by Paola Russo at Just One Eye—I love Paola and everything she touches."

The sun goes down and the store fills with soft light, reflecting off the glass to create rooms within rooms. A silver gelatin print by Man Ray is repeated in reflection; handcrafted wooden vitrines display gleaming vintage jewelry, and mid-century furniture multiplies into geometric patterns. In the courtyard, the heat of the day is retained, and the faint sound of traffic could be rustling leaves. The surface of the water is still; a palette of gray to black, broken by warm spotlights and the knotted branches of a banyan tree.

"Los Angeles is a quiet city," says Ashley. You may or may not agree. But The Row captures something at the heart of the metropolis. A dance between outward display and inward identity, personal expression and unspoken depth. This dance has its own beauty, and no two steps are the same.

———

THEROW.COM

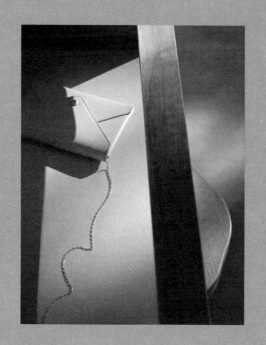

ESSAYS

MY LOS ANGELES

by GREG CHAIT

photos by JUSTIN CHUNG

Greg Chait is the founder of luxurious, laid-back cashmere brand The Elder Statesman, founded in 2007 in Los Angeles. With a flagship store in West Hollywood, its sweaters and blankets are interwoven with the city's relaxed West Coast culture. He lives in Paradise Cove, Malibu, with his daughter, and works at his factory and office in Arts District in Downtown LA, where the brand's collection is produced.

I knew I was going to be in New York or Los Angeles. That's where the music was. I had read a bunch of biographies of people who were successful in that world, and they all started in the mail rooms of either William Morris or CAA—the big ones. So that's what I wanted to do when I graduated college: I would start in the mailroom of a major talent agency.

I arrived in LA from Arizona with my best childhood friend in a U-Haul. We were both blind and refused to wear glasses. The two of us just drove around not knowing where we were. When we finally hit Wilshire we thought we must be on the right track. We had no idea just how big the damn street was.

For a while, I lived on a friend's couch in the South Bay. I got a job in the mailroom of a talent management company called The Firm. They don't pay you much to be in those mailroom programs. That's part of the deal, you really have to want it. They weed out the ones who don't. After I was hired, I moved into a motel in Venice Beach where I stayed for about four months. I paid nightly. It was not at all first-rate. I loved it.

See page 94 for information on The Elder Statesman·

Back then we'd make a giant bowl of pasta at the beginning of the week and then remix it each night. I ate a lot of Grape-Nuts. Watermelon, too. The wife of my first boss at The Firm owned Giorgio Baldi, and sometimes I'd get to go there. It was funny, I was so broke and eating at the best restaurant in the country. Dover sole. That was my order. It's still my favorite restaurant.

Growing up, I thought that LA would be like something out of a Bret Easton Ellis novel, and it was. My first friend here was someone I knew back at the University of Arizona. He was from LA, and his family's house had this *Less Than Zero* vibe. I went to shows at the Viper Room. I was really in Hollywood.

It was an exciting time. I arrived at the height of The Firm's success. You had the Yorns doing their thing with management and production, and The Firm was starting to buy brands. The company was at the forefront of what we now know as "branded entertainment." When I was offered an opportunity to come out of the mailroom to work on that side of the business, I took it.

The arc of a person's career really interests me. That's something I've always paid attention to. I saw the people who had become successful at record labels and in management, and realized that life—even at the top—was not the one I wanted for myself. I liked music too much to work in it. When I was still at The Firm, I began working part-time with Ksubi, a denim brand/art gang out of Australia. The way they put stuff together was really pure. It was about product, making things. I was drawn to that. When they offered me a partnership, I thought, "I don't know what this road is going to look like, but these guys are having a ton of fun." That's how I chose to switch careers. That decision eventually led me to launch my own company, The Elder Statesman, in 2007.

This is a place you can live multiple lives. Los Angeles is unique. It's one of those few cities in the world where anybody can reach their full potential, no matter what industry they're in. I'm in the fashion world but I don't consider myself in fashion. I make things. LA is a great place to do that. It's created brands that are impactful and individual—brands like Rick Owens and Rodarte and The Row. I think it comes down to the landscape itself. It's so spread out; you can have your own existence and your own ideas. In New York and Paris, you're living and working on top of each other. Here, it's like you're on islands.

ELDER-STATESMAN.COM

MY LOS ANGELES
by JOHN ZABAWA

photos by JUSTIN CHUNG

John Zabawa is an artist and graphic designer living in LA, having moved from
Chicago, where he lived for ten years. He was born in Colorado, and grew up in
South Korea and Missouri. As well as painting, he designs album artwork, book
covers, and posters, and works on other freelance projects. His work favors bold
colors, natural forms, and spontaneous expression.

I knew it when I landed on the tarmac at LAX. It felt right. I grew
up in the Midwest and never ventured too far from it. Fall would
come in and turn the trees gold, but the buildings there were cohesive,
the colors monochromatic, despite that hazy orange glow. In LA,
the straight edges and symmetry of the buildings are broken by an
incredible abundance of flora. Most people come out here for the
weather; LA may be laced with opportunity, but it's the sun and
seasons that have the greatest impact on your spirit.

I've been here since 2018. As a painter and visual artist, I would say
LA has a color palette you cannot find anywhere else. It touches
upon those fundamental principles of color, composition, and form
in an almost quintessential way. It's certainly had an effect on my
work—I believe that moving to a historically creative environment
was always going to do that, but with the soaring palms and fantastic
light, it's easy to see why people are drawn here.

Early on I stopped trying to put LA into a bubble or compare it to
other cities. It's very much its own thing. Hispanic and Latin history
is ever present in the buildings and communities. The downtown area
has an industrial feel, then there are the local neighborhood boroughs,
the nightlife, Venice Beach, and Sunset Boulevard. It's so eclectic
that it often doesn't feel like a city, more like a giant collection of
neighborhoods. If you're creative and ambitious, there are endless
places to explore. That's the light and dark of this place—not to

STILL LIFE—INK & ACRYLIC ON PAPER (2019)

SUN—PAPER CUTOUT (2019)

STONES—CYANOTYPE (2019)

mention how much of a distraction the sun is—yet the eclecticism is what speaks to me. My mom used to tell me, "Just choose one thing." Plenty of legendary artists and creative people did just that. But LA gives me the energy to explore everything. At home, I have music equipment, books, and drawings on the floor. It's hard to rein it in, and I'm not sure I want to.

When you move somewhere new, you're always faced with questions about who you are. It's profound to be out of your comfort zone. I surprise myself every day. Moving here has catalyzed the evolution of my work, and I'm still settling into the city's rhythm. It takes time to fully experience a new environment, to learn new ways and form new habits. I've always stayed up late. There's something about working at night, with some jazz or bebop, bossa nova or classical playing in the background. It's an escape, and when I feel most at home. But LA is at its most beautiful in the early morning, so I make more of that time than I used to. From my little cottage, just off Echo Park Lake, I can see all of Echo Park and Silver Lake, and when the sun rises all those peachy hues light up. Everything glows. I make a pot of coffee, read the news, and tend to the garden. It helps me prepare for the day.

I always have something going on in my head, some anxiety about something, but LA has given me a sense of peace, a sense that it's OK to slow down, reflect, and rest. At times, it feels impossible to move fast here. You're surrounded by trees and palms, and greenery overflowing from neighbors' yards or along the street—right now, the city's as green as it has ever been. Nearby are empty deserts, lush forests, and serene beaches. For me, this reasserts an instinctive harmony with nature, which deepens my connection to the world around me and brings me a lot of joy.

———

JOHNZABAWA.COM

A ONE & A TWO:
RICHARD AND DION NEUTRA'S VDL

words by JARED FRANK

photos by MARISSA MARINO

If Richard Neutra's VDL hadn't burned down in 1963, it would stand today, with the Schindler House, as the greatest of Los Angeles's early-modern residences. In both style and philosophy, the clean, mechanical, straight-backed, Apollonian VDL provided a powerful counterpoint to Schindler's earthy, hand-built, low-slung, Dionysian commune, where Neutra first lived when he moved to the West Coast.

Neutra was kicked out of the commune after he stole Schindler's best client, Philip Lovell, for whom he designed the Lovell Health House—a sunlit and humane masterpiece, whose publication launched Neutra's international reputation. Dutch industrialist C. H. van der Leeuw (VDL) flew to LA expressly to tour the Health House, and afterwards asked to visit the architect's home. During the Great Depression, work was scarce and Neutra was staying in a rented bungalow. VDL reached for his checkbook and offered a sizable donation. But with his head held high, Neutra instead negotiated a loan with interest.

Neutra named the VDL after his benefactor, and from the beginning envisioned his personal residence as a research laboratory where he could solve the problem of designing modern homes for families with modest means and limited land. Like a shipbuilder who accounts for every inch, he used space sparingly and efficiently. And presaging the Case Study Program, he convinced manufacturers of prefabricated materials to donate their products for free. In this manner, he constructed a handsome "machine for living" at a cost of 8,000 USD in 1932 (around 150,000 USD today).

His neighbors must have been shocked to witness a little factory rise on the bucolic shores of the Silver Lake Reservoir. Where their homes lay low, Neutra built up to capture commanding views of the lake. Where their interiors remained dark, his opened to sunlight. Where their roofs peaked, his lay flat, available for sunbathing and entertaining. And where they had lawns, he built up front, leaving an open backyard (which he later divided into two courtyards with the addition of a garden cottage).

The façade featured rows of ribbon windows over long strips of stucco. To the left of the entrance, Neutra toed the property line. While to the right of it, his façade graciously stepped back, except for one stucco band, which continued its horizontal movement to become a playful portico over the front door. Neutra prized the clean line, repetition, and precision. The International Style had arrived in Los Angeles, and for the next thirty years Neutra's work demonstrated how it would grow and blossom in the California sun.

In 1963 at the age of seventy-one, Neutra was no longer a partner in an active firm, but an elder statesman who lectured more than he built. When a fire destroyed his home, he was devastated but determined to rebuild. Already committed to multiple speaking engagements, he asked his son, Dion, to spearhead the reconstruction. The VDL 2 that stands in the original's footprint is a family affair and demonstrates how the Neutras' philosophy evolved over the years.

In 1932, Neutra was still designing like a European who prized the minimalist machine aesthetic over all else. But by 1963, he was a Californian who valued the lived experience over the plan. He was now primarily concerned with connecting us to nature via direct and seamless transitions between indoors and out; while also blocking out all that might intrude on that relationship, including noisy roads, unsightly neighbors, and the midday sun. If this led to greater spatial complexity and less pristine compositions, so be it.

Where the VDL 1 featured views of nature, the VDL 2 actually lets us access the outdoors. At every level, there are patios, courtyards,

and reflecting pools, which bring the reservoir's placid surface close. Where the VDL 1's windows remained regular and rhythmic, the VDL 2's shift height to open to the lake, or block the neighbors, or frame the mountains. Where the VDL 1 rarely broke the box, and created drama when it did, the VDL 2 overwhelms with constant alterations in space and ceiling height, and multiple ways to enter and exit every room.

Dion added a "nautical" rooftop funnel and aluminum "airplane-wing" louvers that would look better on one of Albert Frey's Jetsonian homes. And his tendencies towards post-war gadgetry and whiz-bang materiality led to clashing tiles, rose Formicas and one-way mirrors that confuse as often as they delight. Still, it's a magical house to explore as you glide in and out with the breeze. When you finally reach the penthouse, I hope the reflecting pools are full, as the illusion of floating on a sunset sea that merges lake and sky is one of Los Angeles's most ecstatic architectural experiences.

Dion Neutra passed away in 2019 at the accomplished age of ninety-three, after a lifetime devoted to architecture and its preservation. The VDL wouldn't exist today without him, but his contributions also make the house a convoluted tribute to his father's legacy. LA's most spare and exacting architect must be understood by visiting one of his most overcomplicated homes. Luckily, the lovely college students who give tours every Saturday from 11:00 a.m. to 2:30 p.m. will clue you in to the building's layered history. Cal Poly Pomona keeps the space alive as a cultural destination with frequent art installations, performance pieces and architectural interventions. The director Sarah Lorenzen, explains, "A house that is no longer used for living, I believe, must be occupied by something else—otherwise it will lose its vitality."

Richard Neutra's prime objective with the VDL was to prove "that new architecture is no passing fashion, and that, unaltered, it could still be good a generation later." VDL 2 proves that even altered, it is indeed still good—and worth a visit, or two.

------

neutra-vdl.org

CHATEAU MARMONT:
OLD HOLLYWOOD GLAMOR

words by SEAN HOTCHKISS
photos by JUSTIN CHUNG

"Who's your favorite author?" the young woman on the stool next to me asks. She offers me a bowl of cold French fries, and pokes her straw into what used to be a Negroni, but is now only melting, pink cubes. All around us the tinkling of piano music.

"Ah, I don't know. Lately Denis Johnson," I tell her. And her eyes light up. "Stop it!" she proclaims, and proceeds to quote the final stanza from Johnson's story "Beverly Home" from *Jesus' Son*. "All these weirdos," she says. ". . . I had never known, never even imagined for a heartbeat, that there might be a place for people like us." She dunks a cold fry in ketchup.

A place for people like us. Johnson had been talking about a hospital for the elderly, the mentally ill, but he could have been talking about the place we're sitting—the Chateau Marmont—a hotel where disappearing in plain sight is encouraged, where the weight of engagements past practically demands you create a little history of your own, a hotel where quoting Denis Johnson's degenerate, vaguely mystic prose seems more than appropriate. The Chateau is a place of stories, after all. And, yes, also of debauchery. I won't bore you with the yarns you may have heard through the years—of Dennis Hopper's orgies, of John Belushi's overdose, Lindsay Lohan's tab, Helmut Newton's car crash, or Jim Morrison's attempt to fly. Everyone of a certain persuasion, famous or not, seems to have a story here. And that's the point. Director Matt Tyrnauer called the Chateau ". . . a no-tell motel with high-thread-count sheets." What is unclear to me is whether the Castle on the Hill, as it is sometimes called, is a case of chicken, or egg—whether the crazy shit happens because everyone knows other crazy shit has happened, and feels

they have to contribute, or if the crazy shit came first. Either way, the energy is undeniable here. To steal a lyric from Atlanta Rhythm Section: *There is Voodoo in the valves.*

I'm up with the sun the next morning. Half awake. In the bathroom of sprawling Room 44, I swing open the big steel windows over the tub, and shower looking east down Sunset Boulevard. I am, in fact, so close to the windows that my left elbow hangs outside as I scrub my head with shampoo. The hot water cascades pleasantly over the sill and down onto the stone walkway below. Drip. Drop. The day is still gray and cool. Later, the trickle of passing cars on the street below will become a deluge, and the breeze will pick up, and the Los Angeles sun will shine. But for now, it is quiet, nestled in these hills. For now, it feels like my castle.

Last night, before I was on the barstool, I'd taken a long walk down the boulevard in the fading light. The evening was warm and full of promise. I walked up the curved, cobbled pathway, past the valets, through the maze of carpeted stairways, and up into the lobby of the Chateau. A bowl of bright red apples greeted me in the dim light. The term "guest" is thrown around loosely in some hotels, but it seems to hold more weight here. The former apartment complex has a broken-in feel—like the crash pad of a hip uncle who likes velvet, and listens to Lou Reed B-sides. Things are a bit tattered, with a few stains on the brown carpet from parties past, sure, but still unmistakably Old Hollywood glam. Hotelier André Balazs bought the joint in 1990, and sacrificed none of the charisma in the renovation. If you crinkle your nose, you can smell the cigarettes, long since smoked; squint and you swear you can see the drugs, long since ingested, on the mirrored surfaces of the powder rooms. It's precisely this mix of both high and low, of European tea salons and skid row, that makes this place work. A writer pal of mine told me he likes to make a pit stop at the old liquor store on the corner of Sunset before each visit to the Chateau. The bottle of Champagne he procures there is enjoyed with his In-N-Out burger and fries. High. Low.

The derelict brand of decadence works. People don't just stay here.

They camp out here for stretches. It's become a bit of a dream for a certain subsection of Hollywood to shack up at the Chateau. Returning patrons request their favorite rooms, arrange trysts, lock in deals, play ping-pong by the pool, piano in the lobby, pen notes on the personalized stationary. Do people even live in hotels anymore? Well, maybe not. But they live here. Fictionally, like Stephen Dorff as Johnny Marco in Sofia Coppola's *Somewhere*—required LA viewing if you haven't seen it—and in real life, too. Emile Haynie's *We Fall*, one of my favorite albums of 2015, was made here. Producer Haynie was recovering from a particularly vicious breakup, living in one of the Chateau's bungalows. Musicians who just happened to be here playing, staying, or partying—Lana Del Rey or Father John Misty, say—would swing by the room and record. As I said before, things just seem to happen serendipitously here. Even art.

There are many different Chateau Marmonts. The Chateau of the visiting businessman who takes his espresso and eggs early in a sunken lobby nook, the whispering elderly European couple with their army of suitcases, and, yes, the actors, writers, models, directors, rockers, and young Hollywood scions who put this place on the map. There is also my Chateau, and yours. All these weirdos. Strangers passing silently in the night like ships. And whatever you do here, however you arrive or leave, whether you stay for a night or a month, you're only a small part of the story, a sprinkling of improvisation on top of an already classic track. One played so loud, and so long, the grooves begin to hiss under the weight of the stylus.

CHATEAUMARMONT.COM

ADDITIONAL INFORMATION

ARCHITECTURE

POINTS OF INTEREST

1   STAHL HOUSE

Pierre Koenig, *1960*. 1635 Woods Dr, Los Angeles, CA 90069.

2   EAMES HOUSE

Charles and Ray Eames, *1949*. 203 N Chautauqua Blvd, Pacific Palisades,
CA 90272.

3   NEUTRA VDL STUDIO & RESIDENCES

Richard and Dion Neutra, *1932 & 1964*. 2300 Silver Lake Blvd,
Los Angeles, CA 90039.

4   HOLLYHOCK HOUSE

Frank Lloyd Wright, *1921*. 4800 Hollywood Blvd, Los Angeles, CA 90027.

5   ENNIS HOUSE

Frank Lloyd Wright, *1924*. 2607 Glendower Ave, Los Angeles, CA 90027.

6   THE GAMBLE HOUSE

Greene and Greene, *1908*. 4 Westmoreland Pl, Pasadena, CA 91103.

7   GRIFFITH OBSERVATORY

John C. Austin, Frederick M. Ashley, *1935*. 2800 E Observatory Rd, Los Angeles, CA 90027.

8   CHEMOSPHERE

John Lautner, *1960*. 7776 Torreyson Dr, Los Angeles, CA 90046.

9   THE BRADBURY BUILDING

Sumner Hunt, George H. Wyman, *1893*. 304 S Broadway, Los Angeles, CA 90013.

10 WAYFARERS CHAPEL

Frank Lloyd Wright Jr., *1951*. 5755 Palos Verdes Dr S, Rancho Palos Verdes, CA 90275.

ART

1   MAK CENTER

Art Center, 1137 S Cochran Ave, Los Angeles, CA 90019.

2   BLUM & POE

Gallery, 2727 S La Cienega Blvd, Los Angeles, CA 90034.

3   NORTON SIMON MUSEUM

Museum, 411 W Colorado Blvd, Pasadena, CA 91105.

4   LACMA

Museum, 5905 Wilshire Blvd, Los Angeles, CA 90036.

5   THE GETTY CENTER

Museum, 1200 Getty Center Dr, Los Angeles, CA 90049.

6   THE GETTY VILLA

Classical Art Museum, 17985 Pacific Coast Hwy, Pacific Palisades,
CA 90272.

7   THE BROAD

Contemporary Art Museum, 221 S Grand Ave, Los Angeles, CA 90012.

8   THE HUNTINGTON

Library, Art Museum & Botanical Gardens, 1151 Oxford Rd, San Marino,
CA 91108.

9   FRANKLIN D. MURPHY SCULPTURE GARDEN

Sculpture Garden, 245 Charles E Young Dr E, Los Angeles, CA 90095.

10   ANNENBERG SPACE FOR PHOTOGRAPHY

Gallery, 2000 Avenue of the Stars, Los Angeles, CA 90067.

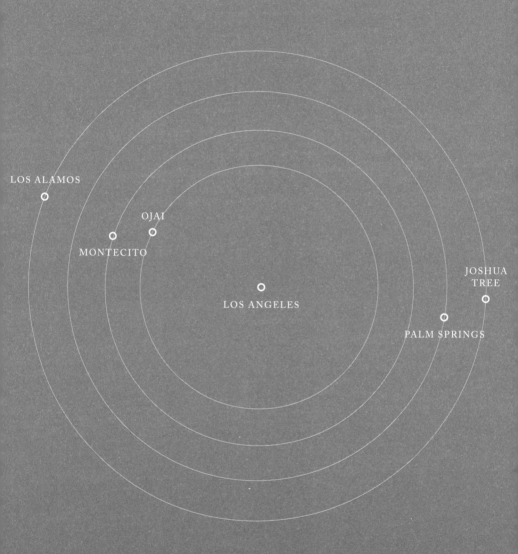

LOS ALAMOS

OJAI

MONTECITO

JOSHUA
TREE

LOS ANGELES

PALM SPRINGS

N

WEEKEND TRIPS

83 miles (133 km)

OJAI
1 hour and 40 minutes by car, or 1 hour and 30 minutes by train, plus 30 minutes by car.

For a peaceful escape to a valley in the Topatopa Mountains, ideal for hikes, wine tasting, and meditation. Check into luxury guesthouse and working organic farm Ojai Vista Farm for a serene stay in the hills.

92 miles (148 km)

MONTECITO
2 hours and 10 minutes by car, or 2 hours and 15 minutes by train, plus 20 minutes by bus.

For a calm pocket of Santa Barbara County. Soak in the warm breezes of the Pacific at Butterfly Beach, or explore the region's distinctive flora at Lotusland botanical garden.

107 miles (172 km)

PALM SPRINGS
2 hours and 40 minutes by car, or by bus.

For Desert Modernist architecture against a dramatic Sonoran Desert backdrop. Stay at L'Horizon Resort and Spa for sleek and relaxing 1950s luxury.

131 miles (211 km)

JOSHUA TREE
3 hours and 20 minutes by car, or 2 hours and 40 minutes by train, plus 40 minutes by car.

For rugged rock formations, stark desert landscapes, and iconic, bristling flora. The one-mile Hidden Valley hike is a good introduction to the area, while Shop on the Mesa and Wonder Valley Oil Shop are both worthy boutiques to explore.

152 miles (245 km)

LOS ALAMOS
3 hours by car, or 2 hours and 50 minutes by train, plus 50 minutes by car.

For an Old West town surrounded by ranches and vineyards in the Santa Ynez Valley. Stay at the Alamo Motel for a modern ranch-style getaway.

THE CEREAL EDIT

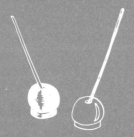

1 RITUAL INCENSE &
POLISHED-BRASS HOLDER SET
FROM BODHA

Therapeutic perfumers Bodha create
scents to promote mindfulness and well-
being. Founders Emily and Fred
L'Ami, a trained perfumer and
designer respectively, produce a
small fragrance collection designed
for calming, purifying and grounding rituals. Their incense is made in
Japan using traditional methods and
organic woods and oils, and has a
smokeless but fragrant burn.

2 INSTANT COFFEE
BY CANYON COFFEE

Canyon's instant coffee, sourced from
Celinga, Ethiopia, is designed for those
emergency situations where a quality
brew simply cannot be found. Each
packet equates to one cup, and can be
kept in your bag for far longer than
freshly roasted beans. You can also
try Canyon's premium-grade organic
beans at Neighborhood Coffee Shop
on La Brea Avenue. We recommend a
V60 pour over, owners Ally Walsh and
Casey Wojtalewicz's favorite way to
drink coffee at home.

3   SPIRIT DUST
     BY MOON JUICE

Amanda Chantal Bacon's brand, Moon Juice, is perhaps best known for its Moon Dust health supplements. Spirit Dust uses a blend of adaptogenic herbs to reduce stress and improve mood. Many of the ingredients have been known in Ayurvedic and traditional Chinese medicine for millennia, and include reishi mushroom extract, ashwagandha, astragalus, mimosa bark, and danshen.

4   ANTI-FIT CREW FROM OLDERBROTHER

Olderbrother is a unisex clothing brand that uses sustainable, natural dyes, such as hibiscus, wood bark, turmeric, and madder root to color their garments, made from Japanese cotton, linen, wool, and woven rice paper. Their organic cotton, pale-blue crewneck sweatshirt is sewn in California, dyed with natural indigo and ashwagandha, and cut in a loose fit. Test out the soft fabric in their small beach boutique on Rose Avenue, Venice.

5   RITUAL SERUM FROM LESSE

Organic skin-care brand Lesse (pronounced "less") fittingly focuses on just three skin-care products: a serum, cleanser, and face mask. Each are made with rigorously researched ingredients, such as algae, jojoba seed, and calendula flower extracts, chosen for their diverse properties that improve the health and complexion of various skin types. Apply a few drops of the serum daily to clean skin—and as it is travel-sized, your skin-care regime can be maintained on the move.

A DAY IN LOS ANGELES

AN ITINERARY

9 A.M. KONBI

Start the day in Echo Park at Konbi for a coffee and French pastry, or one of their celebrated Japanese sandwiches, such as the layered omelette with dashi, mayo, and dijon mustard. *See page 70*

10 A.M. COUNTER-SPACE

Head up to Counter-Space on Hyperion Avenue to check out their eclectic combination of mid-century furniture and high-quality, everyday clothing in tones of white, beige, navy, and black. *See page 86*

11 A.M. HOLLYHOCK HOUSE

Take a short cab ride to Hollyhock House to explore the gardens and interiors of the Mayan Revival home designed by Frank Lloyd Wright. Positioned on a green hill in East Hollywood, the house affords views of the Griffith Observatory in the distance. *See page 126*

NOON MARU COFFEE

A twenty-minute walk up North New Hampshire and Franklin Avenues will bring you to Maru Coffee's Los Feliz location, where you can recharge with a pour over or espresso from a hand-thrown ceramic cup in a calming space. *See page 74*

1 P.M.	**JON & VINNY'S**
	For lunch, take a thirty-minute cab ride west to the small neighborhood restaurant Jon & Vinny's in Fairfax for a slice of LA's finest pizza. Make a reservation in advance, or simply turn up—you can always grab a takeout if the tables are full. *See page 66*
2:30 P.M.	**SUMNER**
	Post-pizza, take a stroll down Melrose Avenue and head to Sumner for a browse of their rare and sculptural selection of twentieth-century furniture. *See page 82*
3:30 P.M.	**THE ROW**
	Also on Melrose, The Row proffers a taste of Olsen-Hollywood luxury. As you explore the clothing rails and handbags, placed reverently throughout the brand's modernist flagship store, be prepared to encounter eye-watering beauty. *See page 94*
4:30 P.M.	**STAHL HOUSE**
	Take a short drive into the Hollywood Hills in time for the evening tour of Stahl House, the mid-century architectural icon, and for its equally iconic views over LA, lit by the late afternoon sun. *See page 142*
7 P.M.	**FELIX TRATTORIA**
	In the evening, drive down to Venice for perhaps the finest pasta in the city, made fresh before your eyes in a climate-controlled, glassed-in kitchen. The exact options change regularly at Felix, but all are sure to delight. *See page 46*

CEREAL PACKING TIPS

OUR SIX ESSENTIALS

TOTE BAG

A lightweight, foldable tote bag is handy when you buy one too many souvenirs and can't fit them all in your suitcase. It's also a great option for carrying your daily essentials as you explore the city.

SUPPLEMENTS

A small pillbox of supplements such as echinacea, vitamins, and Korean ginseng can prove useful when on the road. Jet lag and changes in temperature and environment can make you feel run-down. It's a good idea to give your immune system a boost!

SCARF

A large scarf will not only keep you warm when it's cold and protect you from the sun when it's hot; it will also double as a much-needed blanket on flights and train journeys. Choose the material of your scarf according to the time of year: linen for warmer months, and wool or cashmere for chillier weather.

SUNGLASSES

The ultimate LA staple has to be a pair of comfortable, good-quality sunglasses. A classic design that suits your face will elevate any outfit, and a high UV filter will protect your eyes from LA's intense sunlight. As Jack Nicholson once said, "With my sunglasses on, I'm Jack Nicholson. Without them, I'm fat and sixty."

MUSIC

Download the Cereal Spotify playlist before you leave! It's the perfect companion for those long-haul flights, train rides, and road trips.

readcereal.com/playlist

ESSENTIAL OIL

An essential oil in your scent of choice is a must. Depending on the oil, it can be used as a moisturizer, facial cleanser, makeup remover, beard oil, bug repellent, and calming meditative ointment.

Rosa Park is cofounder and editor in chief of Cereal. She travels extensively for the magazine and was inspired to create a series of city guides that highlighted her favorite places to visit. Cereal is a biannual magazine known for its original take on design, style, and travel.